Islamist Movements

Protégées of the Ayatollahs

Table of Contents

Title Pages

Dedication Page, Foreword, and Caption

Chapter One: Islamic Republic of Iran Revolution, State Sponsorship of International Terrorism, and Oppression at Home and Abroad

Chapter Two: Islamic Republic Testing of Ballistic Missiles, Sanctions on Terrorism, Nuclear Monitoring, Verification, Detection, and Resolve

Chapter Three: The Way Forward—2016 and Beyond

Dedication: *To the legacy of Diana Davis Spencer for her interest in pro-democracy dissidents*

Foreword

The photo depicts a November 3, 2004 portrait of Ayatollah Khomeini; President George W. Bush is standing next to Khomeini; the photo also shows a shackled effigy of the Statue of Liberty displayed outside the former American embassy in Tehran to mark the anniversary of the U.S. hostage crisis after the mission was stormed by students acting under the auspices of the Islamic Republic of Iran; this study considers them as "Islamists," following an ideology that introduces Islam into the political sphere. [1]

The juxtaposition of Khomeini and Bush is the epitome of Khomeini's oft repeated mantra that, "America can't do a damn thing," to hurt Iran.

Amid the euphoria of the 1979 Iranian Revolution, the Islamic Republic held 52 Americans for 444 days, and Khomeini described the embassy as a "nest of spies." This choreographed drama led to severing of diplomatic ties in 1980. *AFP Photo/Behrouz Mehr, credit to Getty Images*

Missing from the photo is Abu Bakr al Baghdadi, forefather of the Islamic State of Iraq and Syria (aka Islamic State). He is only one of the several protégées of "Khomeinism," whether he realizes it or not. Al Qaeda is another. As Islamist descendants of the Iranian regime, this study discusses them but more importantly focuses on the main threat—a toxic mix of the Bashar Assad regime in Syria, Iran, and Hezbollah.

This foreword provides an occasion to present the backstory argument followed by a glimpse at the bottom line as we look through and past 2016.

In the wake of the 9/11 attacks against American targets and with no state since Turkey was dismantled, journalist Yaakov Lappin wrote a book called *Virtual Caliphate*. He reasoned that al Qaeda, which saw itself as a government in exile along with its hundreds of affiliate organizations, had failed to achieve its goal of reestablishing the caliphate.

Failure to create a homeland necessitated the formation of an unforeseen and unprecedented entity—that is, a virtual caliphate—an Islamist state that exists on computer servers around the world.

In *Virtual Caliphate*, Lappin showed how Islamists, equipped with twenty-first-century technology to achieve a seventh-century vision, hoped to upload the virtual caliphate into the physical world. By 2013, Lappin turned his attention away from al Qaeda and focused on a Shiite axis composed of the Assad regime, Iran, and Hezbollah, which he argued was a greater threat than either a virtual or physical caliphate of al Qaeda. [2]

It is true that the main threat is the Assad regime, Iran, and Hezbollah. Meanwhile, *AFP* reports planning for a well-coordinated European-wide 9/11 type attacks. [3] Counterterrorism officials are finding indications of sleeper cells comprised of citizens from European nations returning from Syria to assault their countries of origin.

In the context of defeating the Shiite axis—Assad regime, Iran, and Hezbollah—well-coordinated European-wide 9/11 type attacks can be stopped before it is too late. Now to the bottom line as we look to and past the year 2016. Tehran plays a "long game" comparable with al Qaeda, which counsels strategic patience. In addition, Islamic State won recruits by promising a truer Islam than that of al Qaeda. Islamic State has an energetic strategy of land seizure now, albeit in stages. These phases are: Expel U.S. forces from Iraq; create a proto-emirate that allows

2

expansion; launch assaults against Syria, Jordan, Kuwait, and Saudi Arabia from the Iraq base; and use the expanded Caliphate to take down Israel.[4]

Phillip Smyth, writing in *Foreign Policy* January 5, 2016, sees the Islamic Republic in a long-term struggle to control the region's Shiite community and counter its main Sunni regional foe, Saudi Arabia. More to the point, Tehran wishes to promote its theocratic absolutism inherent in velayat-e faqih. This concept forms the basis of Iran's clerical rule, and "Islamist Resistance" ideologies.[5]

So, the Iranian regime believes the clock is on its side. The nuclear deal with the major powers should yield funds from sanctions relief that can be used to reinforce its nuclear and conventional military capabilities, transfer more arms to proxies in Syria, missiles for Lebanon (Hezbollah) and Gaza (Hamas), and send additional arms to proxies in Iraq.

Posing as a normal state, the Islamic Republic uses heated language against Israel, builds up its offensive missile capability, ramps up illicit missile tests, continues to sponsor terrorist assaults against civilians, and launches attacks against the prodemocracy Iranian opposition without fear of retribution by the West. Iran has a history of carrying out covert attacks overseas; hence, Iranian proxies might target Riyadh's diplomats as in the foiled plot during October 2011 to kill its Washington Ambassador and now Foreign Minister—Adel al-Jubeir.

The Assistant U.S. Attorney, Southern District of New York, filed Five counts of conspiracy, including Conspiracy to Murder a Foreign National (Adel al-Jubeir of The Kingdom of Saudi Arabia to the United States of America,) October 11, 2011. Moreover, on a number of occasions, Tehran's agents have assassinated Iranian opposition figures in European capitals.

"Right to enrich uranium on Iranian soil," an outcome of the nuclear talks, provides the Islamic Republic undeserved legitimacy as a nuclear power and an ability to intimate other regional actors, such as the Arab Gulf States.

Finally, in view of Implementation Day of the nuclear deal with Iran on January 16, 2016, it falls on parliaments in the West to keep their executive branches from appeasing the Iranian regime—permitting it to test ballistic missiles, using terrorism, and violating international norms of human rights.

3

Chapter One: Islamic Republic of Iran 1979 Revolution as Inspiration for Islamist Movements and Ways to Counter Islamic Republic and its Islamist Protégées

Islamic Republic of Iran Revolution, State Sponsorship of International Terrorism, and Oppression at Home and Abroad

Islamist Movements

> Islamic State of Syria and Iraq (aka, Islamic State)
> Core Al Qaeda
> Al Qaeda in the Arabian Peninsula (AQAP)
> Jabhat al-Nusra
> Hezbollah in Lebanon
> Hamas in Gaza

Defeating the Shiite axis—Assad regime, Iran, and Hezbollah— to stop well-coordinated European-wide 9/11 type attacks

Countering Islamist Movements with the Syrian National Coalition (SNC), especially Free Syrian Army (FSA) to Counter Islamists in Syria

National Council of Resistance of Iran, particularly Mujahedeen-e- Khalq (MEK)/ People's Mojahedin Organization Of Iran (PMOI) to Counter Islamists and Iranian Regime Proxies in Iraq

Fear of Soft Revolution to Counter Islamic Republic

Arab League Council of Foreign Ministers to Counter Islamic Republic

Saudi Arabia vs Khomeinism via Islamic Revolutionary Guard Corps (IRGC)

Just let it sink in: Without success of the founder of the Islamic Republic in creating a terrorist state, Islamist movements would not have been inspired to seize land for their own terrorist states. The 1979 Revolution of Iran spread to Sunni Hamas in Gaza and Shiite Hezbollah in Lebanon and reflects the expansion of extremist, religious-based ideology.

In its theology, there is something quite unique about Islamists. There is a totalitarianism in waiting not found in other Abrahamic faiths like Judaism and Christianity—a total submission and commitment to God. The Islamic State carries this submission way over the top, at the expense of moderate Muslims, who often are expected to bringing Islamists to heel.

The Islamic State was preceded in 1999 by Abu Musab al Zarqawi; he had already been planning world domination for much of the decade. He adopted a seven-step plan for establishing a caliphate, an explicitly Islamist empire with authority over all Muslims and domination of the region. He envisaged toppling regimes in the Middle East, which would create the vacuum for the Caliphate.

Zarqawi's goal was to create war between two major sects of Islam, his own Sunnis and the "apostate" Shiites. The fall of Saddam Hussein left Sunnis vulnerable. After the demise of Saddam, many secular "Saddamists" rightly feared reprisals from Shiites and hurried to Zarqawi's Islamist alternative.

In late 2004, al Qaeda in Iraq came into being, and Zarqawi pledged allegiance to Osama bin Laden. Yet Zarqawi quarreled incessantly with al Qaeda over tactics and targets. That same year, Ayman al Zawahiri—then a top al Qaeda official and now the group's leader—wrote to Zarqawi asking him to stop beheading hostages and killing Shiites, which was alienating Muslims and harming the image of Islam. Zarqawi boldly and with scant respect declined.

By 2006, Zarqawi's group controlled large chunks of Iraq's Anbar province, the huge Sunni region that makes up the western part of the country. In October of that year, the group declared itself to be the Islamic State of Syria and Iraq (Islamic State). Its announcement of a new caliphate precipitated a final break with al Qaeda.

Core al Qaeda formed in or about 1989 as the base mainly in Pakistan and Afghanistan; it continues to refrain from state-building for an incremental approach to world domination. By the end of 2013, Islamic State controlled Raqqa, Syria, as its capital. It then focused on northwest Iraq, capturing Fallujah in 2014 and later Mosul. At one point, the caliphate claimed land from Raqqa to about 60 miles from the Iranian border in Iraq's eastern Diyala Province. This area is about the distance from where a group of moderate Iranian Shiites resided as opponents of the Iranian regime.

How to defeat the Shiite axis—Assad regime, Iran, and Hezbollah—to stop well-coordinated European-wide 9/11 type attacks? Partner more with Sunni Kurds in Syria; create a safe zone for them along the Syrian-Turkish border; in quiet alignment with Israel, target Hezbollah in Syria; and help the Saudi-financed coalition of mainly Sunni dissidents against Assad.

The Assistant U.S. Attorney, Southern District of New York, filed Five counts of conspiracy, including "Conspiracy to Murder a Foreign National (Adel al-Jubeir of The Kingdom of Saudi Arabia to the United States of America,) October 11, 2011. Moreover, on a number of occasions, Tehran's agents have assassinated Iranian opposition figures in European capitals. With the above history in mind, note that Islamic State competes and cooperates with al Qaeda. They are friends and enemies. Inspired by Iran, Islamic State and al Qaeda are friends and enemies and sometime collude against common enemies as in an old Arab Bedouin saying:

> I, against my brothers, I and my brothers against my cousins, I and my brothers and my cousins against the world.

As friends, an al Qaeda affiliate, Jabhat al-Nusra (JN), operates in Syria and has a behind-the-scenes accord with Islamic State and Iran's proxies like Hezbollah so that all can assault the American-supported Free Syrian Army (FSA). Both the Syrian and Iranian regimes used al Qaeda affiliates to derail the Syrian Revolution toward sectarianism and thereby justify military actions against unarmed Syrian protesters with the beginning of the Arab rebellions in 2011 for Syria.

As enemies, Iran supports Bashar Assad in Damascus, but Islamic State and Jabhat al-Nusra fight to depose him. Islamic State is a threat to the Islamic Republic along the Iranian border with Iraq. Al Qaeda in the Arabian Peninsula (AQAP) formed in 2009 as a union between the Yemeni and Saudi al Qaeda branches and is a threat to regional states, including the two countries that were the locale of the merger.

Al Qaeda core remains weak and did not conduct attacks of consequence in 2015. If there were a European-wide 9/11 style assault, all bets are off. For now, however, the al Qaeda ideological wallop is on the decline in contrast to affiliates like AQAP and JN, which possess a bigger punch. The same is true for Islamic

State; it disregarded al Qaeda and withdrew, which would have been inconceivable during the reign of Osama bin Laden.

To help friends against their enemies, Tehran is trying to keep Islamic State from establishing a foothold in Yemen and is poised to go all in to support Yemen; a former Islamic Revolutionary Guards Corps (IRGC) Commander in Chief and now member of Iran's Expediency Council praised the leader of Yemen's al Houthis in an open letter of March 30, 2015; he laid down a moral commitment that this study believes might be followed with arms. [6]

Though on the rise, AQAP has lost leaders via American drone strikes. But those deficits may be offset by return of key al Qaeda lieutenants from Iran. They had been under house arrest there. In *Not By Sanctions Alone* for The Washington Institute for Near East Study (TWI), Michael Eisenstadt argued that Tehran may have released al Qaeda members to thwart a "soft revolution" spearheaded by sanctions relief that would undermine the 1979 Revolution. The logic of the Eisenstadt reasoning: Sanctions relief from complying with the nuclear deal is a backdoor to the downfall of the Revolution by allowing westerners to enter Iran and change the mindset of the populous. [7]

Regarding Iranian dissidents in Iraq I headed a fact-finding delegation there in 2008 for the *Iran Policy Committee*, (now known as *Iran Policy Committee Publishing*). [8] Our aim was to interview Sunni Awakening members, moderate Iraqi Shiites, as well as Iraqi and American officials and the Iranian opposition. The dissidents included members of the Mujahedeen-e Khalq (MEK) in Camp Ashraf, Iraq.

In interviewing Sons of Iraq, I met tribal chiefs who were adamant that without American military protection they would be vulnerable to attack by Iranian-sponsored Shiite militias in Iraq and Islamic State fighters. Some even preferred to defect to al Qaeda of Iraq rather than to be killed by Shiite militias sponsored by the Iranian regime. [9]

Khamenei also gave lukewarm support to the deal, saying Washington would use the accord to try to sabotage his country's Islamic Revolution. "We won't allow American political, economic or cultural influence in Iran," the 76-year-old supreme leader said in August 2015, according to Jay Solomon in the *WSJ* of January 8, 2016. [10]

Eisenstadt had penned his July 2013 report for The Washington Institute for Near East Policy; he stated that Khamenei often echoes Khomeini's frequent warnings about a cultural invasion. While Iran's natural defenses and geographic depth pose significant obstacles to an invasion, its population is unprotected against the foreign "cultural invasion" of huge concern to Khomeini and Khamenei.

Large segments of Iranians have stopped accepting the ideology of the 1979 Revolution; moreover, each person is susceptible to subversive messages that enter the country via the Internet, radio, and satellite television. Hence, the Iranian regime goes to great lengths to create strategic depth in the information domain.

In addition to insulating Iranians not a part of the ruling elite from outside influence, the regime also tries to export the Revolution abroad. On December 28, 2015, *Fars news Agency* reports that Khamenei's top adviser for international affairs Ali Akbar Velayati renewed Tehran's stance in support of oppressed people and resistance movements in the region.[11]

Trend online magazine out of Baku, Azerbaijan provides evidence in support of a theme of this study that Tehran is exporting its Revolution to its version of the "near abroad," e.g., to regional states like Saudi Arabia and Yemen: Velayati said in mid-December 2015 that the Islamic Republic's influence spreads from Yemen to Lebanon.[12]

While seeming to care about the oppressed abroad, the Iranian regime engages in a crackdown against minority Sunnis at home. Sunni political prisoners in Gohardasht (Rajai-Shahr) in the last week of 2015 published an open letter titled "the last cry."[13]

"We would like to inform you that following a series of executions of Sunni youths in recent years, this time the Iranian regime intends to execute all the remaining death-row Sunni prisoners in Rajai-Shahr Prison." Their letter urged fellow Iranian Sunnis and religious leaders to condemn and prevent this "historic crime." The meaning is clear. The regime issues crocodile tears in favor of oppressed abroad while preparing to executive minorities at home.

With respect to exporting the 1979 Revolution, it is not only Khamenei's top adviser for international affairs who makes very aggressive statements. President Rouhani's special aide for the affairs of ethnic groups and religious minorities, former Intelligence Minister, Ali Younesi, praised ancient Iran and its widespread empires at the beginning of March 2015. He reminisced about the "great Iran"

8

including nations within Iran's plateau from China's borders to the Gulf, a consequential signal that Iranian transnationalism rages in the Islamic Republic.[14]

Rouhani's special aide proclaimed that people now living in neighboring countries are also Iranian because their countries were separated from the "great Iran's" east and west. "Iraq is not only within the area of Iran's civilization, it is also Iran's identity, culture, and capital and this is true now, as in the past." [15]

In other words, Iraq is but a satrap (province) of Iran. (This study chooses the term satrap because of its ancient Greek and Persian origins, which seems appropriate to the situation.)

At an International Islamic Unity Conference in Tehran on December 27, 2015, Rouhani called on Saudi Arabia to review what he called its hostile policies against Muslim countries, particularly against Bashar Assad of Syria. [16]

The import of this Rouhani doublespeak is to allow Assad to remain in power and continue using barrel bombs against those who oppose him, rather than transitioning out in favor of a coalition of opposition groups. The Iranian regime views the ousting of Assad as a strategic setback.

Fars reports that a meeting occurred in Riyadh on December 10, 2015, in which Jaysh al-Islam and other oppositionists participated. Lina Khatib, a Senior Research Associate at the Arab Reform Initiative placed a post on the *CNN* website about two high-level dissidents in that group, which Saudi Arabia favors.

For good reason, Khatib said that the killing of its top leader, Zahran Alloush and his deputy a few days after the December 10 meeting raises serious concerns about the future of planned negotiations between the Syrian regime and the opposition, casting doubt over the regime's intentions.[17]

The opposition had initially wanted to use Jaysh al-Islam as an alternative to the Syrian National Coalition (SNC), ultimately paving the way for claiming a leading political role in Syria in the post-Bashar al-Assad era. Jaysh al-Islam, however, had begun cooperating with the SNC when its top leaders were killed, either by a Syrian regime or Russian airstrike.

Khatib's bottom line is correct: Assad's strategy is to achieve a scenario in which the two remaining actors in Syria would be the regime and Islamic State. Such an unfortunate turn of events would eliminate the negotiations scenario altogether;

Assad could argue that the choices were then either his secular regime or an Islamist movement (Islamic State), which served the ideological and national interests of the Iranian regime in keeping Assad in power.

According to Dennis Ross, in *Politico Magazine*, on January 10, 2016, Assad consciously made Syria into a sectarian conflict, believing he could survive only if the Alawites, and other minorities, saw their survival depending on his. Thereafter, the conflict transitioned into a proxy war mainly with Saudi Arabia and Turkey against Iran. The subsequent vacuum was filled by Iran, Hezbollah, and Iran's other Shia militia proxies; Saudi Arabia, Turkey, and Qatar; Russia; and Islamic State.[18]

Fars reports that a couple of days after Syrian regime or Russian airstrikes in Syria, a spokesman for the Iranian Foreign Ministry denied a claim made at an Arab League Council of Foreign Ministers that Iran was interfering in internal affairs of Arab states. The spokesman said, "Unfortunately, some countries [Saudi Arabia and its Gulf allies], which have been under fire as main suspects of supporting extremism and terrorism, are trying to play the blame game on others and proceed with the policy of depicting Iran as a threat." [19]

On Jan. 3, 2016, Max Boot, of the Council on Foreign Relations, wrote a post in *Commentary Magazine* that called Saudi Arabia an American ally of necessity.

Boot is spot on in holding that, "Distasteful as the Saudis are, the Iranian regime is far worse. The Saudis are not carrying out crimes against humanity the way that Iran is. And Saudi Arabia is not seeking to subvert its neighbors or to make war on America or our allies. Indeed, Saudi Arabia has reached a quiet rapprochement with Israel because the two states are united in their mutual opposition to growing Iranian power." [20]

Tehran, isolated from the Arab states, vainly sought to divert the attention to Israel as the main threat to the region, which the Arab League did not accept.

With return of Khomeini to Iran in 1979, the Revolution inspired Shiites in Saudi Arabia's Eastern Province to rise up, but only briefly. Khomeinism had planted the seeds for the Islamic State to rise. A theocratic power in the neighborhood with pretenses as a transnational leader for all Muslims was a threat to the Saudi role as custodian of the two Holy Mosques—Mecca and Medina.

Other regional actors include Yemen where Iran seeks to topple a regime supported by Riyadh and Washington. And the story is even more complicated because Islamic State has operatives in at least eight provinces of Yemen and challenges al Qaeda in the Arabian Peninsula (AQAP). It formed in January 2009 through a union of the Saudi and Yemeni factions in Yemen and worldwide.

Actions of Tehran to spread Khomeinism provided oxygen for rise of Islamic State; Iran's narrative compares favorably—a borderless caliphate—with the storyline of Tehran, which is also a world without frontiers. The Islamic State and al Qaeda of Iraq take advantage of Iranian-inspired dissatisfaction with Baghdad and endanger Sunni and moderate Shiite Iraqis in places like Fallujah, Ramadi, and Mosul. Islamic State is a threat to Kurdistan Muslims as well as Kurds and Syria's Muslims and minorities. Its threat extends to Egypt via Libya and the Sinai Desert.

On January 6, 2016 Reuters reported that attacks by Islamic State militants on Libya's biggest oil ports started fires that spread to five large oil storage tanks. [21]

Islamic State has taken advantage of chaos to expand its presence in Libya. [22]

In a February 2009 article, Mehdi Khalaji, a Qom-trained Shiite theologian, at The Washington Institute for Near East Study (TWI), stated that, "Iran has maintained informal ties to the Muslim Brotherhood for many years, and Shiite Islam probably has more appeal among Egyptian Sunnis than it does among Sunnis in other Arab countries." [23]

Khalaji describes how Iran's supreme leader Ayatollah Ali Khamenei became interested in political activities after meeting a Muslim Brotherhood intellectual who played a major role in connecting Shiite Islamists to militant movements, irrespective of whether they were Shiite or Sunni prior to Iran's Revolution of 1979.

After the army overthrew Muslim Brotherhood Egyptian president Mohamed Morsi on July 3, 2013, Shiite Iran and Shiite Hezbollah began seeking closer relations with the Sunni Brotherhood. On November 27, 2015, the *Middle East Research Institute TV Monitor Project* quoted a Jordanian intellectual as saying, "ISIS [Islamic State] is not that different ideologically from the Muslim Brotherhood." [24]

It is revolutionary ideology that infuses terror with religion that needs to be addressed. That ideology already ruled in Iran prior to the rise of Islamic State and abetted its ascent. Now, Tehran acts like Moscow during the Cold War. So long as the Communist Party was holding sway in the former Soviet Union, no fights against communist groups anywhere in the world were effective in eliminating them.

Regarding the link to the nuclear deal with Iran, the new Cold War discussed above is heating up between Iran and Saudi Arabia. Writing in *Foreign Policy Voices*, Kim Ghattas *BBC* correspondent covering international affairs states on May 7, 2015 that, "While the Obama administration may hope the nuclear deal paves the way for a more peaceful Middle East, it just may convince Riyadh to turn its conflict with Tehran up a notch." [25]

So the year 2016 opens with a war of the embassies involving Tehran and Riyadh, and the Ghattas forecast is occurring in surreal time. Moreover, *AFP* reports that Iran's supreme leader Khamenei said on January 3, Saudi Arabia would face "divine revenge" for executing a top Shiite cleric whose death sparked protests in which the Kingdom's embassy in Tehran was firebombed. Officials in Iraq, Lebanon, and Syria condemned the execution of the cleric, Nimr al-Nimr, who spent more than a decade studying theology in the Islamic Republic. He was a driving force behind anti-government protests in Saudi Arabia in 2011, in the east of the country. [26]

What makes the new Cold War so dangerous is that Riyadh views itself Guardians of the Holy Places Mecca and Medina on the Peninsula and Al-Aqsa Mosque in Jerusalem, a trio of venerated shrines in the Islamic world. Iran, however, accuses Saudi Arabia of killing Iranian Pilgrims during the Haj and forfeiting any legitimacy as guardians.

Fears intensified in Riyadh that Arab revolts in Tunisia and Egypt might also topple the Kingdom and its Gulf allies in the region. The United Arab Emirates and Bahrain defended their Saudi Sunni ally with words of support and diplomatic actions. Such executions were necessary to confront extremism by either Shiites backed by Iran to spread its Islamism in the Gulf or Sunnis of the Islamic State.

Taking a cue from Khamenei regarding the execution of al-Nimr, during the first week of January 2016, other officials of the regime piled on. Ayatollah Ahmad

Khatami, a member of the Assembly of Experts and a Friday Prayer leader, denounced the execution as a "crime" by Saudi Arabia's "infamous regime." The Islamic Revolutionary Guards Corps (IRGC) issued a statement that the Saudi government would pay a "heavy price" for "this shameful act," which was a sign of the "decay" of the Saudi rulers. [27]

Saudi Foreign Minister Adel al-Jubeir announced on January 3, 2016 that Saudi Arabia would cut diplomatic ties with Iran, in the fallout after Riyadh's execution of the opposition Shiite cleric prompted outraged protesters to storm the Saudi Embassy in Tehran. The Minister said that all Iranian diplomats must leave Saudi Arabia within 48 hours. His Ministry announced that by condemning the execution, Iran had "revealed its true face represented in support for terrorism," "blind sectarianism," and "by its defense of terrorist acts," Iran was a "partner in their crimes in the entire region." [28]

The meaning of the intensification of the Iranian-Saudi Cold War is that it places Washington in a heck of a pickle. On one hand, the United States would like to keep Tehran on board the nuclear deal. On the other hand, Washington seeks to be an ally of Riyadh and others in the region looking for backing against the Iranian threat. The White House walked a fine line in neither mentioning the nuclear topic nor addressing the specific person executed by Riyadh. On January 4, 2016, *The New York Times* quoted Ben Rhodes—National Security Adviser—as saying that Washington had been complaining to the Saudis for years about human rights issues. [29]

Minister al-Jubeir had asked during a September 2015 interview with *Al-Hayat* given on the sidelines of the UN General Assembly meeting in New York, whether Iran is a "state or a revolution," If it wants to dominate the region with its ideological brand, "we cannot deal with it." [30]

In a comparable vein, see *Guardians of the Revolution: Iran and the World in the Age of the Ayatollahs* (2009) and a post in *The National Interest*, (September-October 2012) by Ray Takeyh. He explains that The Islamic Republic of Iran is different from its revolutionary counterparts In that, "the ideology of its state is its religion." [31]

Khomeini believed that vitality of his Islamist vision at home to be contingent on its relentless export abroad. In this regard, Takeyh holds that, "Iran's foreign policy would be an extension of its domestic revolutionary turmoil." Like Islamic State, God's vision was not confined to a single nation. [32]

Tehran aids Sunni Hamas because it serves the purpose to counter Israel, a democracy that is the ideological antithesis of Iran. Tehran is misogynist, flouts the rule of law, and oppresses minorities; Jerusalem treats women and men equally, practices rule of law handed down through the ages to the Jewish people, and adheres to majority rule with minority rights for Arabs, Christians, and others.

Tehran supports Shiite Hezbollah in Lebanon because it serves the Iranian regime's regional agenda. These priorities are a combination of ideology and interests. There is evidence that ideology trumps interests for regimes like Iran. Tehran also kills its moderate opponents in Iran, who are primarily Shiite. [33]

Likewise, Islamic State is a terrorist movement that is not only hell-bent on killing Shiites; it also seeks to gain territory and power by eliminating all those standing in its way, i.e. the primarily Sunni-Syrian opposition referenced above. Ironically, Islamic State and Bashar Assad refrained from targeting each other. To the contrary, Assad and Iran support Islamic State in battling the Syrian opposition.

Not to go unmentioned are Iran's Islamic Revolutionary Guard Corps (IRGC) in Iraq and Tehran's proxies like Hezbollah in Syria backed by Iran's Quds (Jerusalem) Special Forces.

Islamic State did not just rise up from hell. Its ascent derives from killing of 300,000 + civilians by the Damascus regime of Assad. His primary sponsor is the dictatorship in Tehran, according to Gen. Jack Keane Chair of The Institute for Study of War. [34]

At a September 29, 2015 Hearing with Members of the House Foreign Affairs Subcommittee on Terrorism, Nonproliferation, and Trade, they questioned Gen. Keane on both Syria and Iraq. He told the panel that the indigenous ground forces in Syria and Iraq are not capable of defeating Islamic State. The United States has no effective ground force, which is necessary to defeat Islamic State. U.S. airstrikes will neither defeat it nor deny this movement to attack at will. Because of its sanctuary in Syria, Washington cannot defeat Islamic State in either Syria or Iraq. [35]

Finally, Keane testified that, "The United States should not coordinate any military operations with Russia. To do so, we are de facto in collusion with the Syrian regime, Iran, the Quds Force, and Hezbollah." In accord with the remarks of Gen. Keane, Tehran exploits the dread of Washington about escalation in Syria. It is necessary to change the calculus of the Iranian regime so that it fears an American ground force multiplier to indigenous forces in both Syria and Iraq. Otherwise, Iran is liable to exploit the Sunni-Shiite divide for its ideological aims.[36]

In agreement with Gen. Keane, Aaron David Miller writing in *Foreign Affairs* holds that Iran is using the rise of Islamic State to consolidate its power in Syria and keep Iraq's Shiites and Assad standing against well-armed and tenacious Sunnis.[37]

The CIA *World Fact Book* for Syria lists Sunnis at 74%; the CIA estimates that minorities include Alawi and Shiites combine for some 13%. [38]

Many Alawites fear that if Assad falls, there will be reprisals by Syria's majority Sunni population, which led protests against Assad during ongoing Arab revolts in the Middle East.

Islamic State targets Alawi as Sunnis, while typical Sunni Muslims have long regarded Alawites as adherents of an obscure, even heretical cult, according to Sam Dagher, *WSJ* senior correspondent who focuses on Syria, Iraq, and Iran. So Islamic State mischaracterizes Alawites and kills them. [39]

What about Iran? Tehran's Shiite proxies provide ground forces for Russian airstrikes to hit Sunni adversaries of the Assad regime; while pretending to fight Islamic State, Moscow targets Sunni civilians opposed to Assad and acts like it is shooting at Islamic State members and leaders. Both Moscow and Tehran know better: Their business as usual "banality of evil" is the height of hypocrisy. [40]

Islamic State is ignorant; the new Dual Alliance of Moscow and Tehran is hypocritical; the West engages in feel-good airstrikes with limited ground force presence against phantom Islamic State leaders and fighters in Syria and Iraq. Such tactics are no way to confront the Iranian regime's sponsorship of terrorism.

Iran as a State Sponsor of International Terrorism

The Department of State *Country Reports on Terrorism* for 2014 specifies that to designate a country as a State Sponsor, the Secretary of State must determine that the government has repeatedly provided support for acts of international terrorism. Once a country is designated, it remains until the designation is rescinded. A wide range of sanctions are imposed as a result of a designation. [41]

Based on data available to *Country Reports* for 2014, Iran had been unwilling to account for senior al Qaeda members it had held in its custody. Iran previously allowed AQ facilitators to operate a core pipeline through Iran since at least 2009, enabling this group to move funds and fighters to Syria.

With newer information, this study made the following inference: Factions within the Iranian regime brought about release of al Qaeda members from house arrest to make sure funds from sanctions relief as a part of the nuclear deal would not be a source for penetration of the country by foreigners. They might spearhead a "soft revolution."

Holding al Qaeda members in Iran was a basis for the designation of Iran as a State Sponsor of Terrorism. Those under house arrest were likely to strengthen the depleted senior ranks of al Qaeda in the Arabian Peninsula. In other words, there is an alternative explanation tied to sanctions relief and the nuclear deal for why Iran released al Qaeda members from house arrest.

Keep in mind the complicated relations among Islamists, Iranian regime, and the major powers; note that some of the same state actors are on stage for the next chapter on sanctions for missiles, terrorism, and the nuclear deal with Iran. They have unresolved. They have unresolved issues that motivate them toward conflict and cooperation. The Islamic Republic of Iran is at the heart of these two chapters, e.g., how the regime's state sponsorship of international terrorism and oppression at home is and should be handled by the major powers.

Chapter Two: Islamic Republic Testing of Ballistic Missiles, Sanctions on Terrorism, Nuclear Monitoring, Verification, Detection, and Resolve

President Rouhani Orders Acceleration of Islamic Republic Missile Testing; Uncovered by Nuclear Deal Consistent with UNSCR 2231, which formalizes the Joint Comprehensive Plan of Action (JCPOA), Adopted July 14, 2015 in Austria

Non-Nuclear Sanctions Testimony of Secretary Kerry regarding Nuclear Deal

UN Security Council Resolution 1929 Prohibitions against Testing in the JPA; the JCPOA largely reflects what was agreed in an April 2, 2015 framework for the accord. It replaces a Joint Plan of Action (JPA) interim nuclear accord in operation since January 2014.

Democratic Senators Letters to Secretary Kerry

Republican Senators Letter to President Obama

Senators Kirk-Cardin Bill in Senate to Impose Sanctions on Iran

Democrats Ramp up pressure on Obama to sanction Iran for Illicit Missile Tests

Nuclear Monitoring, Verification, Detection, and Resolve

The *Wall Street Journal* published an article on December 29, 2015 that the United States plans to impose new sanctions on Iran after the Islamic Republic tested ballistic missiles in violation of United Nations Security Council resolutions. [42]

According to *PressTV*, President Rouhani announced the next day that he is ordering the defense ministry to accelerate development of its missile program. [43]

Rouhani viewed the plan by the White House as a measure in line with what he called "hostile" U.S. policies to "illegally interfere in the Islamic Republic of Iran's programs for boosting the defense power."

Rouhani said that Iran's missile power, which he described as a means to protect the country's sovereignty and a major deterrence against terrorism in the Middle East and the world, had never been up for negotiations, including in the nuclear talks with the P5+1 group—the five permanent members of the UN Security Council plus Germany—which resulted in the JCPOA in Austria on July 14.

Rouhani held that the development of ballistic missiles was "conventional and important" to his nation's defense. He also claimed that Iran's missile program is not covered by the nuclear deal. In a July Senate hearing, however, Secretary of State John Kerry said Iran had agreed that non-nuclear sanctions imposed by the United States would not violate the terms of the nuclear deal. [44]

On December 11, 2015, a United Nations experts' panel reported that Iran's attempted procurement of Grade 5 titanium alloy bars had been in violation of resolution 1737 (2006). [45] On the same day, Reuters reported that Iran's October launch of a test of a medium-range Emad rocket had violated United Nations Security Council Resolution 1929. [46]

That resolution of June 9, 2010 prohibits Iran from undertaking "any activity related to ballistic missiles capable of delivering nuclear weapons, including launches using ballistic missile technology, and that States shall take all necessary measures to prevent the transfer of technology or technical assistance to Iran related to such activities." [47]

Security Council resolution 1929 remained valid until the nuclear deal was implemented on January 16, 2016, according to White House excerpts from the Department of Treasury. A key statement in the excerpts is that U.S. statutory sanctions focused on Iran's support for terrorism, human rights abuses, and missile activities will remain in effect and continue to be enforced. [48]

On January 17, 2016, the U.S. Department of Treasury Office of Foreign Assets Control (OFAC) sanctioned 11 individuals and entities responsible for supporting Iran's ballistic missile program. [49]

In announcing the sanctions, Adam Szubin, U.S. acting undersecretary for terrorism and financial intelligence, said Iran's ballistic missile program poses a significant threat to regional and global security, and it will continue to be subject to international sanctions.

According to Iran's *ISNA* news agency via *Agence France-Presse*, Tehran's foreign ministry countered that Iran's missile program has never been designed to carry nuclear weapons, and the sanctions against Iran's ballistic missile program have no legal or moral legitimacy. And according to the Islamic Republic News Agency, (IRNA), Tehran's defense minister said new U.S. sanctions on Iran's missile programs indicates that the United States through hostile policies and enmity tries to weaken Iran's defense power but to no avail. [50]

It might be up to the Congress via the venue of hearings to shed light whether Treasury continues to sanction individuals mentioned above or ceases due to the drumbeat of criticism from Tehran.

Also related to Iran's compliance with sanctions in the post-Implementation period is an analysis by former IAEA inspector and colleagues at the Institute for Science and International Security. They considered the latest report by IAEA and penned an Implementation Day Report, January 17, 2016. David Albright, Andrea Stricker, and Serena Kelleher-Vergantini conclude that:

"Iran has made it clear that it has no intention of complying with missile and arms restrictions in new United Nations Security Council resolution 2231 or national restrictions of supplier countries…It is imperative that the U.S. government and its allies impose missile-related sanctions on Iranian and other entities as soon as possible in order to show that the United States will strictly enforce the UNSC resolution and JCPOA." [51] The Treasury announcement cited above is the first step in meeting the Albright et al suggestion.

This study concurs with the bottom line of the analysis above but believes the Obama administration may lack the will to continue to impose its sanctions in the area of ballistic missiles. If not, it would be up to the U.S. Congress to do the heavy lifting as it did in initiating sanctions against Iran in the first place. Another twist in the Iran saga and Capitol Hill concerns North Korea.

Simon Henderson of The Washington Institute for Near East Policy is an expert on the Gulf. On January 6, 2016, Henderson mused about the meaning of possible transfer of Iranian technology to North Korea. "Confusing as it may be for diplomats seeking to ease tensions in the Middle East, the relationship between Tehran and Pyongyang should not be considered a separate issue," according to Henderson. [52]

With Tehran's links to Pyongyang's missile technology, Iran may be able to access nuclear weapon skills as well, e.g., transferring its technologies for enriching uranium for Pyongyang's plutonium extraction equipment from spent nuclear fuel. North Korea has maintained a close and long-term relationship with Iran on transfer of missiles and missile-related technologies. It appears as if such missile transfers would violate UN sanctions on both Tehran and Pyongyang. In view of Implementation Day of the nuclear deal with Iran on January 16, 2016, it may fall to the U.S. Congress to explore links between Iran and North Korea.

Links between Iran and North Korea are significant in part because of the assertion by Pyongyang that it had tested a thermonuclear device.

Irrespective of the validity of that claim, the import of the test may be relevant to miniaturization; it is a way to place a small nuclear weapon on a missile using any type of plutonium, including reactor-grade without degradation in performance, according to two nonproliferation experts, Victor Gilinsky and Henry Sokolski. They wrote on January 18, 2016 in the *WSJ*, "The Other Dangers from that North Korean Nuke Test."

Gilinsky and Sokolski warn that, "Scoffing at Pyongyang's hydrogen-weapons claims ignored new, dangerous potential developments." Plutonium produced in nuclear-power reactors could become available as weapons material is a danger, especially if Pyongyang decided to sell its new weapons technology to a country like Iran. [53]

Hark back to the pre-Implementation Day period: Iran had carried out a new medium range ballistic missile test in breach of two United Nations Security Council resolutions, a senior U.S. official told *Fox News*. On December 7, 2015, Fox reported that the missile, known as a Ghadr-110, has a range of 1,800–2000 km, or 1200 miles, and is capable of carrying a nuclear warhead. The missile fired in November 2015 is an improved version of the Shahab 3; the new one is similar to the precision guided missile tested by Iran on October 10, 2015, which brought forth strong condemnation. [54]

The first launch prompted a group of eleven Democratic senators to write a letter of October 21, 2015 to Secretary Kerry expressing concern over Iran's ballistic missile program. [55]

The delayed reply gave rise to a letter of December 9, 2015 from two Republican senators to President Obama. Senators Kelly Ayotte (R-NH) and Mark Kirk (R-IL) reiterated concerns regarding lack of U.S. response to Iranian ballistic missile tests. The letter emphasized that the Iranian regime's advanced missiles posed a threat to the United States and its friends in the Middle East. [56]

Some of President Obama's closest Democratic allies in and outside the Senate joined Republicans in calling on the administration to reverse course and sanction Iran for illicit missile tests. Democrats included Party Chair Debbie Wasserman Schultz (D-FL) and six other House Democrats wrote a letter of January 6 to President Obama. It urged the administration to act "immediately" to penalize Tehran.

The letter stated that the United States and our allies must take immediate, punitive action and send a strong message to Iran: Violating international laws, treaties, and agreements will have serious consequences.[57]

On April 29, 2015, Treasury Secretary Jack Lew said to The Washington Institute (TWI), "Make no mistake: deal or no deal, we will continue to use all our available tools, including sanctions, to counter Iran's menacing behavior. Iran knows that our host of sanctions focused on its support for terrorism and its violations of human rights are not, and have never been, up for discussion. The Treasury Department's designations of Iranian-backed terrorist groups and the Iranian entities that support them, most notably the IRGC-Qods Force, will persist, giving us a powerful tool to go after Iran's attempts to fund terror."

Commenting on the statement by Secretary Lew, Matthew Levitt of TWI stated on January 1, 2016 that, "Many U.S. allies in the Middle East and a share of the U.S. public have been skeptical that the Obama administration would risk undermining the nuclear agreement by sanctioning Iranian entities over support for terrorism, human rights abuses, or ballistic missile activities." [58]

In fact, however, the Obama administration did place new sanctions against Iran as Secretary Lew indicated. Now that the administration has leverage to hold Iran accountable at issue is whether it possesses the will to do so over time in view of the incessant pushback from the Iranian regime.

When Iran scheduled ballistic missile tests a month after the nuclear deal was announced in July 2015, Iran's semi-official *Fars news agency* claimed on August 13, 2015 that these tests would reinforce Iran's interpretation of UN Security Council Resolution 2231. [59]

UNSCR 2231 formalizes parts of the nuclear deal and calls Iran to refrain from testing ballistic missiles. But President Rouhani said that Iran was unwilling to "abide by any resolution" that would limit its capacity to develop or acquire the weapons it deemed necessary, as reported by *Reuters* on August 22, 2015. [60]

What is the significance of the debate among Rouhani, Obama, and the U.S. Congress on ballistic missiles? The varying interpretations of obligations did not result in the JCPOA agreed to in Austria on July 14, 2015 from taking effect on Implementation Day, January 16, 2016. However, the disputed understandings offer the Congress a point of departure for how to improve the nuclear deal in the post-implementation period.

Rob Satloff of TWI offers several ways to make the deal work better. Prior to Implementation Day, Satloff proposed that the administration could take action on many proposals without reopening negotiations with the Iranians and the Permanent Five Members of the UN Security Council plus Germany (P5+1) group of world powers. [61]

The issue is not whether the powers possess the tools to use against the Iranian regime; they do. Unresolved, however, is whether they have the will to continue to use that leverage. And here is where the President's vision of the world is relevant.

An underlying theme of President Obama's final State of the Union on January 12, 2016 was that American military capabilities would deter and coerce: There would be little need to engage U.S. forces en masse. What is missing from the Obama vision, however, is resolve. [62]

Satloff suggests several options on which the President might reflect. [63]

Since Satloff made his recommendations on August 13, 2015 in *The Atlantic*, the administration has taken action on some of them and ruled out others. This study paraphrases him and places in brackets the state of play for these suggestions.

- **Consequences:** Repair a glaring gap in the agreement, which offers no clear, agreed-upon penalties for Iranian violations of the deal's terms short of the last-resort punishment of a "snapback" of UN sanctions against Iran. The solution is to reach understandings now with America's European partners, the core elements of which should be made public, on appropriate penalties to be imposed for a broad spectrum of Iranian violations. They might range from delaying access for international inspectors to suspect sites, to attempting to smuggle prohibited items outside the special "procurement channel" that will be created for all nuclear-related goods, to undertaking illicit weapons-design programs. The Iran deal gives the U.N. Security Council wide berth to define such penalties at a later date, but the penalties have no value in deterring Iran from violating the accord unless they are clarified now.

[The clarifications have not occurred, suggesting lack of commitment to risk taking such actions.

The JCPOA contains a mechanism for the "snap back" of UN sanctions if Iran docs not satisfactorily resolve a compliance dispute. According to the JCPOA, any veto-wielding member of the UN Security Council would be able to block a UN Security Council resolution that would continue the lifting of UN sanctions despite Iran's refusal to resolve the dispute. These provisions are included in UN Security Council Resolution 2231.

[See Kenneth Katzman and Paul K. Kerr, *Iran Nuclear Agreement*, December 15, 2015]

> **Deterrence:** Reach understandings now with European and other international partners about penalties to be imposed on Iran should it transfer any windfall funds from sanctions relief to its regional allies and terrorist proxies rather than spend it on domestic economic needs. U.S. and Western intelligence agencies closely track the financial and military support that Iran provides its allies, and will be carefully following changes in Iran's disbursement of such assistance; these new multilateral sanctions should impose disproportionate penalties on Iran for every marginal dollar sent, e.g., to Hezbollah in Lebanon Assad in Syria. Because the sanctions are unrelated to the nuclear issue, they are not precluded by the terms of the nuclear accord.

[No visible action taken, suggesting lack of will to take the actions.]:

> U.S. sanctions that are not required to be suspended in accordance with the JCPOA are those sanctioning Iran's support for terrorism, its human rights abuses, and worldwide arms and WMD-related technology to Iran.]

[Indeed, with the onset of Implementation Day, January 16, 2016, Treasury did take action consistent with the Satloff ideas: The Department imposed new sanctions on Iran for persons responsible for supporting Iran's ballistic missile program. Reauthorization by the Congress of the *Iran Sanctions Act*, (ISA), which is separate from nuclear-related sanctions, might be in order.

ISA was enacted in 1996 mainly to deter major foreign energy companies from subscribing to oil and gas field development projects in Iran. Amendments expanded its authorities to prohibitions against a wide range of areas, including supplying to Iran WMD-related technologies.

Additionally, designation of Iran as a state sponsor of terrorism set off a wide array of sanctions against Tehran. Section 13 of ISA states that, "This Act shall cease to be effective on December 31, 2016." So as Kenneth Katzman

says in his piece for the *Atlantic Council* in June 2014, ISA sunsets at the close of year 2016. [64]

That legislation is the basis for the main sanctions against Iran. The Obama administration suspended the secondary sanctions so foreign companies would not be penalized for certain trades with Iran, and it can enter the international banking system; without congressional consent, however, the executive branch cannot lift the primary ones.

ISA gives the administration the authority to terminate sanctions against Iran if all of three criteria are met: Iran has stopped efforts to design, develop, or acquire a nuclear explosive device, chemical, or biological weapons, and ballistic missile technology; Iran has been removed from the list of state sponsors of terrorism; and Iran poses no significant threat to U.S. national security or allies.

Also, the Comprehensive Iran Sanctions, Accountability, and Divestment Act of 2010 (CISADA) adds another layer of complexity to any decision to lift sanctions against Iran.]

- **Pushback:** Ramp up U.S. and allied efforts to counter Iran's negative actions in the Middle East, including interdicting weapons supplies to Hezbollah, Assad, and the Houthis in Yemen; designate as terrorists more leaders of Iranian-backed Shiite militias in Iraq that are committing atrocities; expand training and arming of the Iraqi security forces and the Kurdish Peshmerga in the north as well as vetted Sunni forces in western Iraq; and work with Turkey to create a real safehaven in northern Syria where refugees can obtain humanitarian aid and vetted, non-extremist opposition fighters can be trained and equipped to fight against both Islamic State and the Iran-backed Assad regime.

[Some action taken, but as Gen. Keane explained there is a gap between western capabilities and the resolve to employ them. If the actions Satloff advocated occurred, moreover, they might be instrumental in helping to thwart a European-wide 9/11.]

U.S. officials acknowledge that Iran and the United States have held bilateral talks on regional issues, such as the Syria conflict, since the JCPOA was finalized, but President Obama has said that the Administration is "not counting on" a broader change in Iranian behavior. Since the JCPOA, Iran has stepped up support for the regime of President Bashar Al Assad and conducted at least one ballistic missile test, suggesting that the JCPOA might not improve prospects for American-Iranian cooperation.

[In this respect, see Kenneth Katzman and Paul K. Kerr, *Iran Nuclear Agreement*, December 15, 2015]

- **Declaratory policy:** Affirm as a matter of U.S. policy that the United States will use all means necessary to prevent Iran's accumulation of fissile material (highly enriched uranium) whose sole useful purpose is for a nuclear weapon. Such a statement, to be endorsed by a congressional resolution, would go beyond the "all options are on the table" formulation that, regrettably, has lost all credibility in the Middle East because of the president's public rejection of the military option.

[No action taken. On January 5, 2016, Israeli Prime Minister Benjamin Netanyahu told former Ambassador Dennis Ross, (who is now at TWI) that President Obama said to Netanyahu that Obama had taken the military option off the table. [65]

Just as Iran will claim that all restrictions on enrichment disappear after the fifteenth year of the agreement, the United States should go on record now as saying that it will respond with military force should Iran exercise that alleged right in a way that could only lead to a nuclear weapon. It is not for the president 15 years from now to make this declaration; to be effective and enshrined as U.S. doctrine; it should come from the president who negotiated the original deal with Iran.

[No Action Taken: By taking the military option off the table, it is hard to imagine President Obama would now say the United States will respond with military force should Iran exercise that alleged right in a way that could only lead to a nuclear weapon.]

- **Israeli deterrence:** Ensure that Israel retains its own independent deterrent capability against Iran's potential nuclear weapon by committing to providing technology to the Israelis that would secure this objective over time. A good place to start would be proposing to transfer to Israel the 30,000-pound, bunker-busting Massive Ordnance Penetrator—the only non-nuclear bomb in the U.S. arsenal that could do serious damage to Iran's underground nuclear installations—and the requisite aircraft to carry this weapon. This alone would not substitute for U.S. efforts to build deterrence against Iran. But making sure Israel has its own assets would be a powerful complement.

[Some measures underway]

Nuclear Monitoring, Verification, Detection, and Resolve

In the January 1961 issue of *Foreign Affairs*, Dr. Fred Charles Iklé wrote a seminal piece entitled "After Detection—What?" [66]

Iklé suggested that, "Detecting violations is not enough. What counts are the political and military consequences of a violation once it has been detected." Having worked with Iklé during 1967 at the Rand Corporation, I heard him restate this theme frequently.

Echoing the Iklé thesis, Dennis Ross, states, "Iran will cheat." [67]

Given Iran's track record, it will likely cheat at the margins to test means of verification and see how it might be able to change the baseline. As preeminent political scientists, Iklé and Ross focus on resolve and commitment. In the case of Tehran, Washington must know not only that it is technically capable of detecting a violation but also that it and the rest of the world will want to react if and when a violation is detected.

And for Iran, we know that the regime will cheat, because of its prior history of doing so. The National Council of Resistance of Iran and its largest unit, the Mujahedeen-e- Khalq, regularly document cheating by the Iranian regime on its nuclear promises and obligations. [68]

There was an October 28, 2008 seminar at the Center for Nonproliferation Studies in Monterey California on the topic of "Evidence from Imagery: The Iran and Syrian Nuclear Programs." [69]

The program assessed the validity of exposures of the NCRI/MEK across several cases. The conclusion was that the revelations were independently validated using open sources and methods. Even if the NCRI and MEK did not have an impressive track record, such human nonstate intelligence from resistance sources is at least of value as a "lead" to compare with state-derived information using other sources and methods. [70]

Chapter Three: The Way Forward—2016 and Beyond

Elections

      United States

      UN Secretary General

      European Nations

      European Parliament

Hearings

Briefings

Concerned about Iran's spread of its "ideological brand" not only in Syria but also in Iraq, there were several hearings and briefings in the House of Representatives and in the Senate. Consider one of them in the House on November 5, 2015 and another in the Senate on December 15. One way forward lies with the Congress.

Among the many Members of the House who spoke at one of the Hearings (November 5, 2015) were Ed Royce (R-CA), House Foreign Affairs Chairman (HFAC); Rep. Ileana Ros-Lehtinen (R-FL), Chairman HFAC Subcommittee on Middle East and North Africa; HFAC Ranking Member Rep. Eliot Engel (D-NY); Rep. Brad Sherman (D-CA), HFAC Ranking Democrat Subcommittee on Asia, Chairman Emeritus Subcommittee on Terrorism.

A first step is for Capitol Hill to use hearings to identify the enemy as militant Islam. Indeed, Members have an occasion to label Islamist movements as protégées of the ayatollahs. That is, Members can recast the threat from simply terrorist organizations to Islamist movements fathered by Khomeini and Khamenei via their connection as Khomeinism—an ideology of exporting the Revolution across borders.

Several Members and witnesses expressed the theme of this study: Abetted by present-day Moscow, Tehran is the epicenter of radical Islam intent on spreading its Sharia-like ideology as was Soviet efforts to spread communism in the Cold War era.

Below are specific ideas for discussion in 2016 and beyond.

Hold Tehran's feet to the fire in legislative bodies in America and Europe, including the EU Parliament, in view of the willingness of executives to appease the Iranian regime.

Take advantage of the Iranian regime's fear of a "soft revolution," spearheaded by sanctions relief that would undermine the 1979 Revolution.

Reassure and strengthen friends in the region, in view of the nuclear deal with Iran.

Reflect on the hearings of the House Foreign Affairs Committee of the *Zero Tolerance for Terror Act*. It is a bill introduced on January 6, 2016 in the

114th Congress (2015-2016) as H.R.4333, by Rep. Joseph Kennedy III, (D-MA. [71]

Signal the USA is reengaging in the Middle East with robust diplomacy backed up with a buildup of forces.

Counter Iran by luring Sunnis away from Islamic State; provide arms and more robust air support for moderate Syrian rebels, while exacerbating the split between Islamic State and Jabhat al Nusra. Such actions might also help stop a European-wide 9/11 assault that could be in the planning stages.

Understand that prison breaks during the Civil War in Yemen since March 2015 gave rise to skilled commanders, giving al Qaeda in the Arabian Peninsula an occasion "to go long" again with attacks like those of the underwear bomber in 2009 and computer printers of 2010. [72]

Though badly damaged by coalition attacks and ideologically as well as physically confronted by Islamic State, al Qaeda would be poised to resume its pre-9/11 capability.

Recognize that al Qaeda training camps are springing up in Afghanistan, perhaps under the leadership of a skilled bombmaker released from house arrest in Tehran. If so, al Qaeda can reclaim its diminished infamy as a transnational threat to the near abroad, Europe, and the United States.

Engage moderate Iranian Resistance to counter the triple team of terrorism—Iran, Islamic State, and al Qaeda; they often work together but also against each other.

Be aware of this study's research in Iraq on the moderate Iranian Resistance movement that rejects clerical rule in Tehran, it finds that the regime makes widespread efforts to insulate youths from the influence of the pro-democracy ideas of the Resistance. [73]

Acknowledge that the Iranian clique sets up expositions in the major cities of Iran; prohibits mixing of ordinary criminals with political prisoners like members of the coalition, National Council of Resistance of Iran; and uses torture and public hangings of NCRI members more than other groups.

Publicize how the NCRI family of organizations, including its main unit The People's Mujahedeen of Iran, more commonly known as the Mujahedeen-e-Khalq or MEK, receives the lion's share of attention and opprobrium than do all other protests groups combined. [74]

Counter the Iranian regime with the democratic procedures of the Resistance, which are the ideological antithesis of Iran. Tehran is misogynist, flouts the rule of law, and oppresses minorities; the Resistance treats women and men equally, practices rule of law, and adheres to majority rule in word and deed.

Assess how the NCRI/MEK Ten-Point plan for bringing democracy to Iran poses a threat to the survival of the clerical regime.

Determine how the Iranian regime reigns as a religious dictatorship while posing as a normal state and the Resistance exposes this façade.

Looking back and beyond, this study goes to press on the anniversary date of the Inaugural Address of President Ronald Reagan on January 20, 2016.

I recall Reagan's words that, "Government is not the solution to our problem; government is the problem."

Likewise, the Islamic Republic of Iran is not the suitable partner for the Obama administration to destroy the Islamic State of Iraq and Syria. Because the heart of militant Islam beats in Tehran, Iran cannot be a part of the solution—it is the problem.

[1] Although this study uses the term Islamist in contrast to Jihadist movements, it draws on insights of Scott Stewart's "Gauging the Jihadist Movement in 2016," *Stratfor, Security Weekly*
https://www.stratfor.com/weekly/gauging-jihadist-movement-2016-al-qaeda-camp

[2] Yaakov Lappin, "Why Israelis See Shi'ite Axis as a Greater Threat Than Syrian Jihadis, Special to *IPT News* September 10, 2013,
http://www.investigativeproject.org/4156/why-israelis-see-shiite-axis-as-a-greater-threat

[3] Michel Moutot, "Security experts fear 'European 9/11' in the coming year—Counterterrorism officials say IS learning from previous attacks, planning simultaneous, multi-country strikes in Europe," January 9, 2016, *Agence France-Presse*
bit.ly/1UUZSMM

[4] Scott Stewart, "Gauging the Jihadist Movement in 2016: The Islamic State Camp,"
Stratfor, Security Weekly, January 7, 2016,
https://www.stratfor.com/weekly/gauging-jihadist-movement-2016-islamic-state-camp

[5] Phillip Smyth, "Iran's Martyrdom Machine Springs to Life—Saudi Arabia's execution of a Shiite cleric has put the Middle East on edge — and set up Tehran for its favorite role," *Foreign Policy Argument*, January 5, 2016,
https://foreignpolicy.com/2016/01/05/irans-martyrdom-machine-springs-to-life/

[6] http://www.criticalthreats.org/yemen/moarefian-mohsen-rezaei-writes-letter-to-abdul-malik-al-houthi-march-30-2015

[7] bit.ly\1ST7UXY

[8] http://iranpolicycommitteepublishing.com/

[9] Raymond Tanter, *President Obama and Iraq, Toward a Responsible Troop Drawdown*,
amzn.to/1Q4cUGK

[10] http://www.wsj.com/articles/nuclear-deal-fuels-irans-hard-liners-1452294637?cb=logged0.8439058009535074

[11] *Fars news Agency*, "Leader's Top Aide Stresses Iran's Irrevocable Support for Resistance Movements," December 28, 2015, on.wsj.com/1JQaGeF

[12] http://en.trend.az/iran/politics/2374357.html

[13] http://www.mojahedin.org/newsen/40384

[14] http://en.trend.az/iran/politics/2374357.html

[15] http://en.trend.az/iran/politics/2374357.html

[16] http://en.farsnews.com/newstext.aspx?nn=13941006000550

[17] http://www.cnn.com/2015/12/29/opinions/syria-assad-jaysh-al-islam-killing/

[18] http://www.politico.com/magazine/story/2016/01/obama-mideast-vacuum-213513

[19] http://en.farsnews.com/newstext.aspx?nn=13941006000343

[20] https://www.commentarymagazine.com/foreign-policy/middle-east/saudi-arabia-american-ally-of-necessity/

[21] http://www.nytimes.com/2016/01/07/world/middleeast/libya-oil-storage-tanks-burn-after-isis-attacks-ports.html?_r=0

[22] http://www.washingtoninstitute.org/policy-analysis/view/egypts-muslim-brotherhood-and-iran

[23] http://www.washingtoninstitute.org/policy-analysis/view/egypts-muslim-brotherhood-and-iran

[24] http://www.memritv.org/clip/en/5209.htm

[25] http://foreignpolicy.com/2015/07/15/the-saudi-cold-war-with-iran-heats-up/

[26] http://www.dailymail.co.uk/wires/afp/article-3382548/Saudi-faces-divine-revenge-clerics-execution-Khamenei.html

[27] http://www.rferl.org/content/iran-execution-/27464819.html

[28] http://www.rferl.org/content/iran-execution-/27464819.html

[29] https://www.bostonglobe.com/news/world/2016/01/03/saudi-arabia-cuts-ties-with-iran-amid-fallout-from-cleric-execution/Gui9ZotUY3YpKSYiUWZrDI/story.html

[30] http://www.al-monitor.com/pulse/politics/2015/10/saudi-arabia-yemen-syria-crisis-relations-disputes-agreement.html#ixzz3oqQUftiB

[31] http://nationalinterest.org/article/all-the-ayatollahs-men-7344

[32] http://nationalinterest.org/article/all-the-ayatollahs-men-7344

[33] http://www.amazon.com/Rebels-Iranian-Dissidents-Raymond-Tanter-ebook/dp/B00D4WO3JA/ref=sr_1_1?s=books&ie=UTF8&qid=1446207721&sr=1-1&keywords=tanter+arab+rebels

[34] http://www.wsj.com/video/opinion-journal-gen-keane-analyzing-the-paris-attacks/789A544F-D506-44FF-BEEC-1CFAAA296BD0.html

[35] http://docs.house.gov/meetings/FA/FA18/20150929/103996/HHRG-114-FA18-Transcript-20150929.pdf

[36] http://docs.house.gov/meetings/FA/FA18/20150929/103996/HHRG-114-FA18-Transcript-20150929.pdf

[37] https://www.foreignaffairs.com/lists/2016-01-13/saudi-arabia-and-irans-forever-fight

[38] https://www.cia.gov/library/publications/resources/the-world-factbook/geos/sy.html

[39] http://www.wsj.com/articles/syrias-alawites-the-people-behind-assad-1435166941?alg=y

[40] http://www.meforum.org/5769/saudi-barbarity-iranian-hypocrisy

[41] http://www.state.gov/j/ct/rls/crt/2014/239410.htm

[42] http://www.wsj.com/articles/obama-administration-preparing-fresh-iran-sanctions-1451507921

[43] http://www.presstv.ir/Detail/2015/12/31/443970/Iran-missile-Rouhani-US/

[44] https://www.youtube.com/watch?v=b0LxsUzGya4&feature=youtu.be

[45] http://www.un.org/press/en/2015/sc12163.doc.htm

[46] http://www.reuters.com/article/us-iran-military-missiles-idUSKCN0S505L20151011 and

[47] http://www.un.org/press/en/2010/sc9948.doc.htm

[48] https://www.whitehouse.gov/sites/default/files/docs/jcpoa_key_excerpts.pdf

[49] https://www.treasury.gov/press-center/press-releases/Pages/jl0322.aspx

[50] http://www.irna.ir/en/News/81925961/

[51] http://isis-online.org/uploads/isis-reports/documents/ISIS_Analysis_of_IAEA_JCPOA_Implementation_Report_17Jan2016.pdf

[52] http://www.washingtoninstitute.org/policy-analysis/view/pyongyangs-posturing-the-iranian-dimension

[53] http://www.wsj.com/articles/the-other-dangers-from-that-north-korean-nuke-test-1453162539

[54] http://www.foxnews.com/politics/2015/12/07/iran-tests-another-mid-range-ballistic-missile-in-breach-un-resolutions.html

[55] http://www.cardin.senate.gov/newsroom/press/release/eleven-democratic-senators-express-profound-concern-over-iranian-ballistic-missile-test-in-letter-to-secretary-kerry-?utm_medium=twitter&utm_source=twitterfeed

[56] http://www.ayotte.senate.gov/?p=press_release&id=2367

[57] http://www.foxnews.com/politics/2016/01/07/dems-ramp-up-pressure-on-obama-to-immediately-sanction-iran.html

[58] http://blogs.wsj.com/washwire/2016/01/01/u-s-sanctions-delay-could-open-door-for-iranian-weapons-violations/

[59] http://en.farsnews.com/newstext.aspx?nn=13940522000529

[60] http://www.reuters.com/article/us-iran-military-missile-idUSKCN0QR07C20150822

[61] http://www.washingtoninstitute.org/policy-analysis/view/there-is-a-path-to-a-better-deal-with-iran

[62] http://www.nytimes.com/2016/01/13/us/politics/obama-2016-sotu-transcript.html?_r=0

[63] http://www.washingtoninstitute.org/policy-analysis/view/there-is-a-path-to-a-better-deal-with-iran

[64] http://www.atlanticcouncil.org/images/publications/Easing_US_Sanctions_on_Iran.pdf

[65] http://www.pbs.org/wgbh/frontline/film/netanyahu-at-war/

[66] https://www.foreignaffairs.com/articles/1961-01-01/after-detection-what

[67] http://www.washingtoninstitute.org/policy-analysis/view/iran-will-cheat-then-what

[68] https://iranpolicycommitteepublishing.files.wordpress.com/2015/02/24-feb-2015-ncri-reveals-lavizan3-at-national-press-club-washington-dc.pdf

[69] https://www.youtube.com/watch?v=JkXbbHMKpHk

[70] https://www.fbi.gov/about-us/intelligence/disciplines

[71] https://www.congress.gov/bill/114th-congress/house-bill/4333

[72] https://www.stratfor.com/weekly/gauging-jihadist-movement-2016-al-qaeda-camp

[73] http://www.amazon.com/Rebels-Iranian-Dissidents-Raymond-Tanter-ebook/dp/B00D4WO3JA/ref=sr_1_2?ie=UTF8&qid=1451613812&sr=8-2&keywords=arab+rebels+tanter

[74] http://www.amazon.com/Rebels-Iranian-Dissidents-Raymond-Tanter-ebook/dp/B00D4WO3JA/ref=sr_1_2?ie=UTF8&qid=1451613812&sr=8-2&keywords=arab+rebels+tanter

www.ingramcontent.com/pod-product-compliance
Lightning Source LLC
Chambersburg PA
CBHW050859290526
45792CB00002B/656